RENTER NATION!

How and Why You Should Own Apartment Communities And Can Do So Without Sacrificing Your Lifestyle.

by

Darin R. Garman

Table of Contents

Chapter 1:   The Investment In Apartment Communities Explained. Simple But Not Easy.   8

Chapter 2:   Why Multi-family Housing Will Surge.   10

Chapter 3:   Population Trends, Wages and Affordability.   15

Chapter 4:   Isolation From Technology.   20

Chapter 5:   The Best Way To Profit As A Passive Investor In Apartment Communities.   24

Chapter 6:   Deciding Which Apartment Community Partnerships To Invest In.   28

Chapter 7:   Demand Not From Just Tenants But Investors.   35

Chapter 8:   The Four Gospels of Apartment Community Investing.   40

Chapter 9:   Using Apartment Communities To Blow Up Your IRA / 401k.   46

Chapter 10:   The Final Word On Apartment Community Investing And Your Financial Future.   50

Dedication:

To Case. I have loved you since I was a kid.

Introduction

I am 51 years old and I am going ALL IN ON APARTMENTS as my top investment. I am not going to make this book a mystery. I won't "pop" this in around chapter 4. No sir, I am going all in on apartments and I think you should too. Even if you have no idea what to do, how to begin or know any of this landlord stuff, or heaven forbid, want to deal with property management you can own your own apartment community and profit handsomely by being its owner.

Many people call me the "Paranoid Banker" not because of my background in owning a bank and sitting on its board of directors but because of how I look at investing. I will go into more detail on this of course in the following pages but for now this is coming from a fellow investor, like you, that wants to maximize their returns and wealth in the short time I have left to do so.

I realize that it would be easy to say that YOU should go all in on apartments as an investment if I did not have my own money invested heavily in apartments. Unfortunately, this is what a lot of books, authors, courses, etc. provide. A lot of advice from people that do not take or follow their own advice.

I remember years ago I attended a sales seminar disguised as "How to Make Money from Government Auctions". The pitch was that "anybody" can get rich by buying items at government auctions for "just pennies on the dollar" and then reselling them at retail prices and therefore banking huge profits. Of course, the catch was that to do this right, fast and in the most profitable manner possible, you needed to buy the course at the back of the room for $795.00. So, I go to the back of the room with every intention on buying this thing. This idea of working from home in my underwear using the phone and a computer sounded great. I wanted to cash in on this you know? It sounded easy…right?

Well, when I finally got to the front of the line to buy the books and cassette tapes (remember I am 51) the main speaker that talked for about 90 minutes on how "EASY" this was happened to be walking behind the clerk that was going to help me. I am not sure what got into me at the moment I saw him, but I got the guy's attention and said that I wanted to ask him a quick question. He obliged and here was my question: "How much property have you bought yourself from government auctions and how long have you been doing this? Can you give me a few quick tips that I should know?" When I asked this, I expected his answer to be vague of course but I was expecting him to tell me AT LEAST a figure in the millions right? Or heck, at worst case in the hundreds of thousands of dollars and maybe even a quick crazy story about his adventures. His answer was…. are you ready for this? "None! I am just here to present the material to you, it is up to you to go out and make some money with it" I was shocked. Just to make sure I was not misunderstanding I asked again, "So, you have not done any of this stuff yourself?" He said, "No, I have not." I was blown away.

Let's just say that I placed my credit card back in my wallet faster than you can imagine and left thoroughly disappointed. Here you had a supposed expert communicating how easy all of this was and had not only zero experience but had never risked one penny of his own money on what he was selling. What the hell??

Yes, I was naïve. I found out that this is the way most of the world works. Lots of advice giving and instructions coming from many people that like to act like the WIZARD but in truth have no experience. It is like asking your Aunt Ruth about how to deal with crocodiles in your backyard when her only experience is seeing one on TV. Bad idea.

But you reader can rest assured that this is NOT the case with me. Over the last 25+ years I HAVE "been there done that" when it comes to apartments. I lay it on the line every day in the world of apartments and what does that mean to you? You will be reading GENUINE REAL WORLD INFORMATION that will ultimately tell you THE WAY IT REALLY IS.

So, hop aboard and find out about this apartment stuff and why if you are age 50 or older this is one of the smartest things you can do, right now, especially in today's investment climate. You will not only find that owning your own apartment property is a hell of a lot easier than you think but just how profitable it will be in the coming years too. I love that "P" word – Profit! Let's make some together using this book, shall we?

Time to have some fun and make some money too!

Darin Garman
The Paranoid Banker and
America's Apartment Investment Specialist

Chapter 1

The Investment in Apartment Communities Explained: Simple But Not Easy

Simply put, you need to be an owner of your own apartment community. The more the better especially if you are age 50 or older.

You could literally read just this one sentence and put this book down and get to work and I believe the financial benefits of doing so in the coming years would be amazing for you.

In future chapters we will explore the reasons why those that invest in and own their own apartment communities will be seeing big payoffs in incomes and returns in the future but for now let's explore the simple but not easy question. Owning your own apartment community.

Again, sounds simple enough doesn't it? Owning your own apartment community? However, this is surely not an easy thing to do. It is not like you can fire up your computer, iPhone or smart phone download an app and own your own apartment community. Why? Why is this the case? I mean why can't it be easy?

Well, it is not easy even though investing in and owning your own apartment community is really nothing new in the world of investing. The main reason for this "difficulty" is because owning your own apartment community is an unconventional investment.

Some would bristle at being asked to entertain the thought of investing in an unconventional investment to be sure, however, the thing to always keep in mind is the following:

UNCONVENTIONAL INVESTMENTS PRODUCE UNCONVENTIONAL INVESTMENT RESULTS.

I don't know about you, but I want to have unconventional investment results. I will go ahead and save conventional investment results for other people but for me, and hopefully you too, the more unconventional my investment results are the better.

After reading just this far are you worried about not knowing much of anything about how to own your own apartment community? Property management? Being a landlord? Dealing with tenants, vendors and contractors? Income taxes? Incorporating? Finding the best apartment community to own? All valid concerns of course but the good news is that we will explore how you can get the results of a seasoned apartment property expert without having to deal with any of this. Being an active owner of your own apartment community without being active in its operations. This is, in my opinion, the true definition of investment leverage and a huge advantage for those of us that have an interest in great investment results but not the work or time to get those results.

So, let's explore together how to use investment leverage and start on the path of taking your investment income, results and returns to places you probably thought were not possible.

Chapter 2

Multi-Family Housing Will Surge

Tenants Are Coming For Years.

They are coming. Year after year more and more of them are coming and they will continue to come.

Who am I talking about?

People. Specifically, people that will want, need and must rent an apartment property. People that choose to rent apartments are called: TENANTS!

There are many reasons why you will see more and more people line up to be tenants but for right now let's cover the top three:

1. Cost of Living.
2. Flexibility.
3. Fading of The American Dream.

COST OF LIVING

For most Americans their daily life consists of living paycheck to paycheck. Sure, you can live paycheck to paycheck and own your own home or condo but for most people their current state of living paycheck to paycheck will keep them renting vs. owning. The problem is cost of living.

Simply put, todays average wages and salaries will not keep up with the typical financial responsibility a person has. Long gone are the days when Dad went to work and provided comfortable living for the entire family while Mom stayed home with the kids. In today's world everyone works. Mom, Dad, Brother, Sister, Uncle. Why?

Because they have too. In most households today, everyone works to make ends meet and each year it gets worse. Each year it costs a little more for that car payment, a little more for utilities, a little more for health insurance, a little more for groceries, a little more for gas, etc. For the average American it is tough to make it and then hopefully be able to save a little money too as well as have some money left over for entertainment and a little fun.

Try to throw in some wild cards like say college tuition and then it gets interesting.

This financial paradigm will continue to get worse not better.

Then in addition to all of this you want to throw in the overall cost of owning and maintaining your own home or condo?

Forget about it.

It is not just about affording the mortgage payment either. You see, a lot of people get hung up on this and believe it is all about just affording the mortgage payment. Obviously, this is important, but it is not the whole story. In addition to a mortgage payment you have all the costs of owning your own home or condominium including insurance, repair, maintenance, upkeep, appliances, carpeting, painting, wear and tear, etc. For older homes the worse this is the case due to ongoing needed maintenance.

Heck, even for newer constructed homes the price per square is unreachable for many because of the high cost of construction and materials.

Even with a condominium you have common area (HOA) fees, and, these common area fees do not go down every year they go up.

So, with all this going in the daily life of the average American what will most people continue to do?

Rent.

FLEXIBILITY

Believe it or not more and more people do not want to "settle down" and live in the same city or even in the same neighborhood for years and years. Being able to move because of personal or career opportunities, no matter what a person's age is, is more and more the norm. Remember in today's world the average person will have seven career moves through their life. Gone too are the days when the goal was to land a great job and plant yourself in the same community for the rest of your life to raise a family. If you are 50 years old (or older) this is going to sound totally opposite of what you have come to know. I am 51 as I write this book and if you are around my age you know that this is what you did. You got a job you loved, you established yourself in the community where the job was, you raised a family in that community and then continued to live in that community until your later years and for many until the end.

Not the case anymore especially with those under 40 years of age. Personal and career flexibility is very important for this demographic because long term commitments in all areas of life are not nearly as important as they used to be. Being able to move is now more important than ever and to do this as conveniently and inexpensively as possible the choice for most now is renting vs. owning.

So, in short, if you are someone that for a variety of reasons wants or needs to keep their life or career options open what will you choose to do?

You Will Rent.

THE AMERICAN DREAM FALLS ON DEAF EARS

Remember the American Dream? Stop anyone under 50 years of

age and ask them what the American Dream is, and you will be shocked to find out that 80% of these people will not get the right answer.

Of course, the answer is owning your home. It is what has been pounded into the public, since I can remember anyway, that you have finally "made it" and are living the dream when you own your own home. But many people anymore do not see it that way nor are they really that interested.

Why is this?

Well, for starters there are the reasons that I already stated that have a lot to do with it of course. In addition, owning your own home does not have the financial payoff that it was once thought to have. It was only a few years ago that millions of people lost money owning their own homes.

You see, it was not that long ago that the belief was you could always depend on your home to be an automatic wealth generator for you. You could lose money in the stock market or any other kind of investment, fall ill, have a financial setback of some kind but you could always depend on your home equity to save the day and make you financially free.

This is not the case today nor will it be the case in the foreseeable future and the thing is people know it. So much so that many now deliberately choose to not own their own home because it is not what it used to be. Not the financial safe haven that so many thought was the case for so many years.

Now, before I go any further, I want to be clear in that I am not saying that people are not buying or building their own homes. Heck, this morning on my way to the office I saw a couple of housing developments progressing nicely. I am not saying the market for owning or building your own home or condo has shut off. It hasn't and in some places, there are very healthy home sales and I think this will continue to be the case, however, the numbers are in. We are a nation of renters and as each year passes more and more will rent vs. own.

You are seeing this aren't you? Look around your market, your city, your town. What are most people doing? What is the trend? Are there more demands for building and owning your own residence, or renting? In most cases you will find the demand is in renting and you will also see that this trend will not subside for a long, long time.

The nice thing about this is this is not secret information only for a privileged few to know about or take advantage of. We can see this happening right in front of us.

Chapter 3

Population Trends, Wages, Affordability and Inflation

At the risk of sounding like I am repeating myself I wanted to take this chapter to briefly talk about the "other" trends you are now seeing that will continue to impact my renting vs. owning analysis.

Let's start with population trends and I will keep this pretty simple and this is per our U.S. Census. If you are over 50 years of age and reading this book, chances are you are an owner of your own residence. If you are under 40 years of age the chances you own your own home are pretty good but now, we are getting close to 50/50 between being an owner and a renter. However, if you are 30 years or younger you are most definitely a renter.

What I have covered in the previous paragraph was meant to be simple and to the point without citing twenty different studies and covering 10 pages of charts and graphs but again, if you do your own research, you will find this to be the case. What I have covered here is not really that surprising so far, however, what if I told you that as all those 30 and under folks grow older, they will continue to be renters for longer periods of time before even entertaining buying their own residence if at all?

Think of it this way. The younger they are not only the more apt they are to be renters, which is not such a newsflash, but it is the longer time frame that many will stay renters is what I want you to consider. That is the key here. More and more of our younger generations will stay renters. Why?

Inflation and Cost of Living Increases.

I have already covered this in the previous chapter, but I wanted to highlight just a handful of things, their costs and how this impacts whether people rent or own. Taking just a little deeper dive.

Cars. Have you seen the prices of vehicles going down? No, they continue to go up and at a very brisk pace and if there is something that most people need it is a vehicle. I realize that many that live in larger cities have transit alternatives but between the big cities is a lot of country and there are a lot of people needing vehicles. If there is one thing that is true American's do love and need their automobiles, but this is where it gets interesting:

The average car payment is over $500 per month and it is going to keep on going up and up.

Then, just add all the maintenance and insurance of those ever increasing car payments and you have a lot of money going out every month to have a car and remember, if we are talking about families there are a probably minimum of two or three cars. In most cases you are easily in the thousands of dollars per month.

Cell Phones/Technology. Everyone has a cell phone and they get them younger and younger adding to the monthly costs earlier. Well you can bet someone is paying for the monthly purchase and service contract for probably not one but an average of two or three phones. It is rare anymore to have a phone over two years of age, so, when those phones are traded in for new ones many times there are additional costs to buying the new phone added to that monthly payment. Plus, the variety of monthly subscription services for other technological related items can be staggering. The newest iPhone that came out at the time I am writing this book was over $1,500.00 and you know that most no one, especially under the age of 50, will go without their phones.

Student Loans and/or Tuition. These costs will continue to rise and so will their monthly obligation. In many cases the monthly payment for a student loan is more than a car payment.

Credit Cards. What happens with most Americans is that at the end of the month there is more month than there is money especially when you consider some of the items I just mentioned. What do Americans do? They use credit cards to shore up the difference. As months go by and the cards are used each month to do this the balances on the cards rise and so do their monthly payments and the balances rarely go down since the interest on those balances is so high.

I mentioned just four items that will continue to drive people to rent. The younger the person the more these four items will impact their ability and frankly their interest in renting. There is a long list of items I did not cover and should have added to this short list, but I used just these four because all of them are what the majority of potential homeowners would face and again this is just four. There are a lot more I could have mentioned but did not.

College Degrees Don't Help

This is one more thing that I find alarming but will lead to more and more renters in the future vs. homeowners. It is more and more prevalent that having a college degree does not get you any real true advancement in wages in America. Think of it this way, how many people do you know that have a college degree, are making student loan payments on that college degree but make under $50,000 per year? The numbers are staggering, and you can believe that this will continue to grow and grow and of course, more than likely, these folks will be renters. There are only about a dozen college majors anymore that provide people competitively higher wages upon leaving college for careers in their field.

Wages high enough starting out and continuing to increase in amounts that would allow an easier transition from renter to home owner. For the person with the social work, business, economics, philosophy, art, English, history and dozens of other degrees are surprised to find that their work once they graduate is usually in an area unrelated to their major and at wages that are much lower than they would have anticipated even if they find a job in their college major. In other words, how many people are you aware of that have college degrees but work at Old Navy, is a waiter at Applebee's or works as barista at the Starbucks? These are $30,000 per year wage jobs and these are people that are paying student loan, credit card and car payments.

Sure, for many these jobs are only temporary until they find the right job in their college major and start bringing in more money, however, what you find more often than not is even if they land a job in their major their starting salaries are not much higher than their full time job at Old Navy. Many also find that they will make more money in other areas like retail, sales or even factory labor of some kind vs. their college major.

So as a result, these folks rent.

The last thing I will mention in this chapter is to simply remind you that the cost of living in America is increasing at an alarming rate vs. wage increases. This does not make people necessarily poor, that is not the picture I am trying to paint, but it does impact their ability to own vs. rent. Even the best-case scenario for many is that they will maybe eventually be able or want to own their own home, however, it will be at a much later age meaning they will rent longer.

Chapter 4

Isolation From Technology

You may find it strange that we have a chapter about technology in a book about investing in apartment properties especially since, as of the writing of this book anyway, the "hot" stocks/investment to own is technology stocks and technology companies.

Why would we want to be isolated from technology?

In most people's minds when the word 'technology' is mentioned mostly what is first thought of are the good things that technology has done for humans and continues to do so and I for one would agree. I am a huge supporter of technology being used to help make your and my life a heck of lot easier. So, I am very PRO technology in every way.

Except along with all the advancements in technology we also must face the tremendous downside that technology brings, which in some cases, can negate the good things that technology has done for the human race.

Maybe that is a little overdramatic, however, this does impact you and your investing in a big, big way.

In terms of what you and I are talking about here in this book specifically is the danger technology poses to investors, mainly, through the easy access to your private information and risk of theft from private investor accounts. This IS one of the huge downsides of technology. Criminals using technology to break into investors accounts and obtaining investors information with the sole purpose of stealing money or at the very least information to sell to make money.

You cannot go a week without reading or hearing a story where a business or person has been ripped off. No one or no business is immune to this. People are finding their life savings zapped out of their accounts, businesses brought to a standstill because of theft due to technology. There is at least a 60% chance that you have already been a victim of theft.

In short, instead of a criminal robbing you at gunpoint they can now sit behind a computer and get the same result. The effects of this are obviously much more magnified the older you are. The older you are and the more you lose (or get stolen) the worse of a problem this obviously is.

With all the risks now in every investment using technology you must think about the downside and what the potential risks could be. This is something that can no longer be taken lightly or not even thought about. This is serious. Again, if you are 50 years or older this is VERY SERIOUS.

This is yet another reason many investors are turning to apartment properties. Isolation from the risks of technology. It is not talked about much nor making headlines, but it is a fact. As strange as it may sound investors should look at apartment ownership and investing because of the isolation it provides you from being scammed, ripped off or your information stolen. Again, the older you are the more important this is and is another reason to get serious about owning your own apartment community. When you read the next headline or see the next news story reported in the news about someone or some company being ripped off again you can feel good that your apartment investment is isolated from this.

Now, to say that this is "THE MAIN REASON" to own your

own apartment community is arguable at best, but investors need to be continually thinking not only rate of return, not only income and not only what kind of investments can help them reach their investment goals they also need to be thinking about PROTECTION! How do we go about protecting our money? How do we go about protecting our assets? Owning your own apartment community provides great insurance from theft through technology.

The way it looks now too is that theft using technology will only get worse not better. You can see every day the race is on to have technology replace humans, paper and ink, mail, etc. The race is on to have all your daily cares of life being operated from your phone or computer. All these items coming are all new portals for the bad guys to steal. We cannot be naive and think that we are winning the war against the criminals as the bad guys are advancing at a faster pace than the good guys. It is just the way it is.

So why take chances? Again, especially if you are in the 50+ age category why would you take these chances with your money when you can isolate and insure that your money will not get stolen, hacked, traded or sold to someone else with you being the victim?

As I mentioned earlier, I know this is another reason investors are moving into apartment communities. Right now, however, you are not seeing this information on the news. You are not hearing about it much, if at all from your friends or acquaintances, but you will. It will start becoming more mainstream for investors to own their own apartment communities not only for income, wealth generation and rates of return but also because of protection and isolation of their money.

You could almost compare an investment in an apartment

community to a safe deposit box – only 10X better with your money isolated and safe from theft. Protected and locked up but instead of only providing protection it will provide fantastic returns in addition.

Though this is not the #1 reason most investors think about parking their money in an apartment community it may for many investors arguably be the best reason.

Chapter 5

The Very Best Way To Profit As A Passive Investor In Apartment Communities

When it comes to passive investment in an apartment community you really have three ways you can go about this:

1. Buy a community and hire a manager to run the community for you.

2. Invest in a Real Estate Investment Trust (REIT)

3. Invest In A New Or Existing Apartment Community Partnership.

Which is the best way to go? The answer depends on your circumstances of course so let's go over these one by one briefly to give you some perspective on what the best for you might be.

Buy a community yourself and hire a manager.

There are a lot of advantages to doing this. First and foremost, you can stay on top of the day to day activities and goings on of the community without having to deal with the daily cares of life stuff that a manager would. In other words, you can keep up with and run the property like a CEO runs a company and has employees carrying out the company directives. This is essentially what you would do if you owned your own community. You would be in touch with management on at least a weekly basis and providing information, feedback and opinions on the operations. You would leave all of the management dealings with tenants to them.

Though under this scenario you would not be getting calls in the middle of the night that your toilet does not work you would still be actively involved in the day to day activities. You would be communicating consistently with your manager and sometimes maintenance personnel and calling the shots. This is not being completely passive but does allow you to own the property and again act as CEO in overseeing and running the operations without dealing with tenants and property operations. I suggest this only for someone looking for something to do as this will take a minimum of 20-30 hours per week if done correctly. This would not only include the daily operations but also things like accounting, bookkeeping, legal, vendors, etc.

Real Estate Investment Trust or REIT

Many investors choose REITS because it is very simple and easy. REITS are companies that you can buy stock in, typically publicly traded companies, that buy apartment communities. You prosper when the company prospers. All you must do is buy some stock in the company and the company does all the heavy lifting for you in terms of owning, running and managing the apartments.

This all sounds good until you realize that you really do not actively own your own apartment community. What? That is correct. Remember, a REIT is a stock. You are buying stock in a company that owns apartment communities you are not buying your own apartment community! Keep in mind that when you own your own apartment community you not only get the income from the property, but you get to take advantage of appreciation, equity build up, depreciation and very hefty tax deductions to boot! When you invest in a REIT all you own is stock certificates in a company. Look, I think REIT's are better than not investing in an apartment community at all, but a REIT does not give you active apartment community owner benefits. You want active apartment community owner benefits. This is one of the main reasons why I feel so strongly about apartment community ownership; it is because of all these benefits! Also, REITS are a Wall Street investment. To get the very best apartment communities you need to stay away from Wall Street.

Investing In A Partnership

Partnership investing can be new or existing. There can be a new partnership formed to purchase an apartment community or more than one community. You can also invest in a partnership that may currently own a bunch of communities and so you decide to join those investors and own those communities that are already under ownership.

Partnerships can be any size too. You can have a partnership with just two investors all the way to 2,000 investors if you wanted.

The main benefit to partnership investing is that you get all the active owner benefits in owning the apartment community without being an active owner. You get the same benefits as if you were overseeing, running, managing and up to your eyeballs in the daily operations of the community without ever having to step foot on the property or talk to any management staff at all. This is huge because now you get a ton more ownership benefits while having a life. All the benefits as if you were there every day running and managing without ever having to lift a finger to do so.

Currently, we have hundreds of investors from all over the US involved in our partnerships for this very reason. They get all the active owner benefits of owning the apartments just like they were here right beside me doing all the managing of property and people but because they are members of our partnership, they do not have to worry about any of this. Not only that but all the bookkeeping and income tax work is also all done for them as well.

This is the perfect way to be a passive owner in great apartment communities. Being able to take advantage of owning your very own apartment community while you do something else never to step foot on the property or deal with any of the management decisions or talking to any tenants, vendors or worrying about things like lawn care, snow removal or capital improvements.

As apartment community investing heats up with what I think will be much higher overall returns for their owners in the coming years this will be the vehicle I would recommend you take a serious look at especially if you are 50-year-old or older. There really is no wrong answer in the three ways I have described in this chapter to own your very own apartment community, however, the ONE WAY that has the potential to get you the highest and best investment benefits is owning your very own apartment community through partnership. It provides the best potential leverage for the investor in terms of investment benefits and the best lifestyle benefits as well.

Chapter 6

Deciding Which Apartment Community Partnerships To Invest In

When it comes to investing in a partnership that currently owns an apartment community (or apartment community's) there are only four main items that need most of your attention before deciding.

Now, these are four biggies, so, don't let the fact that I only mention four make you think this is something you can take lightly. It is not. These four are super important in terms of making sure you have a winner investment.

Step One: Aligning The Apartment Community With Your Investment Goals.

The first is making sure you understand what it is you as an investor are trying to achieve. Yes, apartments are going to be the place to be investing but we want to be sure we are investing in the right apartment property.

For example, some apartment partnerships may focus on capital appreciation or large property value increases. This may be a partnership that plans on purchasing an apartment community with the intention of doing some capital improvements over the next 12 – 18 months and then putting it back on the market to sell. During this 12 – 18 months there may be little if any distributions while the work is being completed. In fact, the only real distributions will start when the work is done. Well, if you are an investor looking for immediate income then this may not be the best partnership for you. However, if you are an investor with some IRA or 401(k) moneys this would be an ideal partnership to be involved in as you would not need the income from the property and your IRA/401(k) would get a nice jump in value, tax deferred, once the apartment property sold.

Another example would be a partnership purchasing an established apartment community that looks to produce a 6 – 7% income return over the next 10 years with a nice amount of appreciation with an overall projected return of 10%. Though this sounds pretty darn good you may be in your early 50's and may be a bit behind in your investing and would need to grow that IRA or 401k account or even your regular moneys more aggressively than this. Or, you could be a conservative investor that is now really emphasizing income and would look forward to this kind of income for the next ten years while your apartments continue to appreciate.

Bottom line is before you decide which apartment property to invest in know what it is you want and need to accomplish to meet your overall wealth and income goals. Remember, apartments are only a tool to get you what you want. I firmly believe that it will be "the tool" over the coming years but again, it is just a tool. So, as you start to review apartment community partnership opportunities make sure you know what it is you are looking for. Again, this is step one.

Step Two: Property Due Diligence.

Step two involves putting your real estate buyers hat on in terms of checking out the property or properties that you will be owning. In short, even though you will be a passive owner you need to act like you are buying the entire apartment community yourself vs. being one of a group of people that will be buying the apartment community. Of course, you will have information from the person that is managing the partnership on the apartment community in question and you will want to make sure you go over all this information. But also, in addition, you should also do some due diligence on your own. Where is the property located? What kind of condition is the apartment community in? What is the tenant mix like? Is what surrounds the apartment community a benefit or a detriment? In short, you want to do your research on the property. I recommend taking an in person look at the community, the surroundings and the city the apartment community is located. Play prospect and act as if you are looking to rent one of the apartments and look around the community. After that take a drive or walk around the neighborhood and area and see what it is truly like.

The good news is that even if you are considering a partnership that is hundreds of miles away from you and travel is not a viable option you can still do a lot of research online and find out information on the property and the area. The combination of some research online and some phone calls can help you go a long way in determining what the community is like.

Once you have done your due diligence, in person or not, you will have a set of questions now that you will need to get answers too. Your next step is then contacting the manager of the partnership and get any of your questions or concerns about the property answered and answered satisfactorily.

A couple of caveats here. First, understand that there is no such thing as a perfect property. There will always be properties with pros and cons, so, the key is to make sure the good aspects of an apartment property override any negative aspects of a property in a big way. Do not think everything needs to be perfect to move forward. It doesn't, but, the good news (of any property) needs to outdo any bad news in a big, big way. Second, if you get answers that you are not comfortable with and/or your due diligence finds the property is not as attractive of an investment as you thought it would be then you need to consider not getting involved and wait for another one. As much as I love apartment investments and feel they are going to be the "go to" investment in the coming years I am not talking about all apartment communities. There will be some apartment communities that you will want to stay away from for a variety of reasons.

After your due diligence is completed and this is a community you feel you would want to own as a partner it is now time to request the partnership documents. This is step three.

Step Three. Company Documents.

In step three the partnership documents will usually consist of the following:

1. A company Operating Agreement.
2. A company Private Placement Memorandum.
3 An Asset Management Agreement.

You want to have a chance to review all the partnership documents and agreements that the partnership has for you to agree to and sign off on to be involved in the partnership. You want to have a copy of these agreements, even in rough draft form, sooner vs. later so you have ample time to review them.

Essentially the partnership documents are the rules and regulations of the partnership. Think of the documents as the owner's manual of the partnership. They outline what you can expect from the partnership and what the partnership expects from you as a partner during the time the apartment community is owned. In short, every question you have about the partnership from when you submit your investment to when you get distributions to when and how do you get out of the partnership is in the documents. The partnership documents will cover from A to Z what it is you need to know and be aware of as a partner.

Take your time in going through these documents and do not be hurried to get through them. Again, as with the inspections you did on the apartment community and the city or area before you invest you are essentially doing more due diligence in reviewing the partnership documents. After you review the partnership documents you will want to formulate a list of questions and get those questions answered before moving forward.   Make sure you are clear on any points that you have questions or concerns about. Make sure that once your review and questions are done and answered you are satisfied with those answers before moving forward.

Step 4: Checking Out Those Overseeing and Running the Partnership.

So, you have done your due diligence on the apartment community, you have done your due diligence with the partnership documents now it is time to do some due diligence on the manager or person that will be overseeing the partnership.

What you are mainly looking for here is someone with experience. You want to be sure that this is not their first venture into managing a partnership that will own an apartment community. A good manager will have a resume of many apartment communities over the years owned and managed. A good manager will also have some references for you to contact as well. I recommend a minimum of three references that you can contact and get information from. These would be references of partners that are currently in another of the managers partnerships, or, was in a previous partnership with this manager.

A few red flag items on potential managers would be:

1. Not enough experience. Track record.
2. Cannot come up with three references.
3. Cannot clearly cover or explain any questions or concerns you have regarding the property or the partnership agreements.
4. Does not communicate with you in a timely manner.

By the way you noticed that I did NOT identify losing money as a red flag. The more experience a manager of a partnership has with owning various types of real estate over the years the more this manager will have some properties that may have lost money and did not perform to expectation. It really comes down to a numbers game. Not every property that this manager has probably had has been a winner and that is ok. You want a manager that has made some mistakes and has learned from those mistakes along the way. You want a manager that can identify through past investments the right properties to own and the ones to avoid. So, do not get too concerned if the manager has lost money in the past. I would even make the argument that if they have not lost any money on any real estate investment at some time, they may not have enough experience.

Bottom line is you must feel good about who you are going to be doing business with. This will be a long-term relationship in most cases, so, it pays to do this work ahead of time.

I recommend using these four steps whenever you get involved in any kind of apartment community partnership. Going through this process each time will not only save you some time but can save you a lot of money and headache in the end. Ultimately, the goal is to make as much money as possible by leveraging someone else's knowledge and experience in owning and managing apartment communities.

Keep in mind that it is always easier to get into a relationship and/or investment than it is to get out of one. The good news is each of these steps is not only easy but does not really take that much time. The short time spent on these steps will help you make as much money as possible while avoiding mistakes at the same time.

Chapter 7:

Demand Not Just From Tenants But From Investors

Where do I put my money?

Where do we put our money?

This is a question that many investors have. I am not only talking about individual investors I am talking about small and large funds, corporations, businesses, etc. The question they ask themselves is where do we put our money?

It should come as no surprise that the ultimate value of an investment really comes down to how much demand there is for that investment. Even though this is a book on investing in apartment communities this is really the case for any investment. Value is based on demand for that investment.

Or in many cases perceived future demand or what I call PFD. Perceived Future Demand.

For example, there are many publicly traded companies today that are operating at a loss. Many technology companies for years operate at a loss. Many start ups operate and continue to operate for years at a loss. Amazon is a great example of a company that lost billions of dollars for years. As of the writing of this book Uber Technologies, the ride sharing company, operates at a loss in the billions of dollars per year. Why? Why would investors, partners, pension funds and private equity companies continue to pour money into these money losing companies?

Because they see future demand and future cash flows and

increases in the company's valuation. It is not what is going on right now it is where these investors believe these companies are headed. So, in truth, their banking on PFD. They must. No investor is going to continue to pour money into an investment if there is not going to be a return of the money at some point or at least a perceived return at some point in time in the future.

What you have started to see is this same situation with apartment communities. You have not started to see it yet as in being obvious to just the casual observer, however, you are starting to see investors start to "stock up" on owning apartment communities in large part due to this. Perceived Future Demand.

Why?

Two reasons really.

One reason (or reasons) have to do with what we have already covered in previous chapters in this book. What we have covered however mainly has to do with the demand from tenants and potential tenants to keep apartment properties not only full but an increase in cash flow the communities will produce because of this demand. The more demand from tenants to want to lease apartments the more apartment communities will be able to raise their rents. As mentioned before we see the line of tenants getting longer and longer as they continue to want to and must rent.

But what we have not talked about yet is reason number two and reason number two has to do with PFD. This reason will allow investors to not only make great returns as they own apartment community, but the real payoff will be when they sell those communities. When these communities are sold, in large part, the sales prices obtained for them will be based on the buyer's Perceived Future Demand for that apartment community. In some cases when an apartment community is sold it may look like the buyer is really overpaying for that community and on the surface you may be right, however, if that buyer believes that they are really buying that community at a discount at the time, then, all parties believe they are the winner.

Here is an example: I put together a small partnership to purchase a 24-unit property in Cedar Rapids, IA. Our partnership agreed to purchase the property for the owners asking price. This was a $795,000 purchase and we did not even negotiate a little bit on the purchase. We agreed, pretty much right after the property was placed on the market, that we would pay asking price. Why in the world would we do this? Why would a guy like me with all my years of experience pay full price for a property that is 30+ years old?

PFD! That is why!

As a matter of fact the appraisal just came in on this property at $830,000. So, we have already banked almost $40,000 on this property before we even take over. Why? PFD. Once we take over and once we get some things cleaned up with the rents and the expenses this will easily be a $1,000,000 property and this will be in large part based on PFD. I am considering placing this property on the market right after we close for $250,000 more than what we paid for it to see what will happen. Though I don't think it will sell right away at that price I do believe we will get some interest, play and even some offers probably close to the $1,000,000 mark.

This small isolated case that I just described is what is coming for apartment communities in general. Investors are looking for places to put their money. They are realizing the current

AND FUTURE DEMAND for apartment communities and what the value of these communities could potentially be in the years ahead, so, they will pay for access to these investments now with the belief that their incomes and values will continue to go up and up. Again, PFD.

This is where YOU make your big money by the way. Always remember your biggest cash flow will come from the sale of the apartment property. Even though there will be good income streams coming to you in the coming years that will probably increase over time it is this demand that will get you a larger than expected sales price on your apartment community thereby giving you one heck of a return.

Caution! I am NOT talking about speculation here. This is not like betting. Of course, in general, I am VERY confident apartments will go up in value but there are still stinker apartment communities to avoid. By doing the work before you invest that I described earlier in the book you should be OK, however, keep in mind that not every apartment community will increase in value. There are still those communities that you want to stay away from. Just make sure you do your homework and chances are if you do you will have fantastic investment success.

Chapter 8

The Four Gospels of Apartment Community Investing

There are four words that, if followed, will give you a great return on your apartment community investment in a short period of time. These four words or GOSPELS of apartment community investing will, in my opinion, really drive demand for apartments now and in the very near future. In this chapter when I am talking about demand I am talking demand from investors to own these properties. The Four Gospels have already been shared in one way or another already but let's bring these together to help crystallize what it is I believe you need to make a great apartment investment.

The Gospels Are:

1. Boring
2. Predictable
3. Insulated
4. Existing

Let's go over the gospels in terms of what I believe investors will want and demand more of when it comes to owning apartment properties over the coming years. Remember, you are going to be selling your apartment community to these investors.

BORING

Give me boring apartment communities! I know, I know, from an investment standpoint this sounds, well, boring! But this IS where the money will be made. In BORING apartment communities. What I am referring to are apartment communities that chug along day after day, year after year at a steady clip. These communities produce income and returns that are, well, boring. Boring properties will be as close to predicting the future as you can get, and this is what investors will want.

Let me ask you, would you rather own a property that is super flashy, with a whole bunch of "hype", "marketing" and "positioning" in order for that property to return as much income and value to the owners as possible...

OR

A property that does not need ANY of these things but still produces day in and day out. A property that will not win any design or environmental awards but will have what most qualified tenants want in terms of location, condition and amenities? You see, there is no reinvention necessary here to be extremely profitable in your next apartment property investment.

Remember, most people will want an affordable place to live.

Does this mean the more flashy or trendy apartment communities won't thrive? No, but why take the chance on untested theories, construction or locations when you absolutely don't have to.

Sure, it is really attention getting to be building a new apartment project in the middle of downtown, or, convert that old warehouse into an apartment community or convert the old hotel into apartments but why risk all this when you don't have to.

Remember... BORING IS BEST!

PREDICTABLE

The term predictable is in and of itself boring. But again, this is where the money will be; in predictable apartment communities. Again, let's do some thinking on this together. Will an investor want to purchase a property that has been predictably running and operating over the years, or, some new high-rise apartment community being built on speculation? The answer is obvious.

A boring apartment community that has predictably run for years and produced income and returns over the years IS where the money will be and that is where I recommend your money goes. Of course, I am not saying that an apartment community that defies predictable will not be successful. Sure, it very well can or could be but again think about what investors will want. What does money look for when it comes to finding a home? The more predictable the more will be paid for the apartment community.

INSULATED

I will get a lot of flak for this, but here goes.

You are an investor looking to invest your pension funds money. You are looking for the best place to park your clients pension funds and you have decided on apartment communities. So far so good.

Then you ask yourself, "Do I want to own a property in a market subject to every three or four years of up and down swings in the rental and or real estate market – is this where my money should be invested?"

There are many markets where you can get large upswings in

property value in short periods of time depending on what is happening in those markets. Many areas right now around "tech" companies are in this boat. As the tech continues to feed the market it drives values up and up at an abnormal rate.

But here is the question....will it always go up? Will you count on this with your money?

You can invest in an apartment community and have a dramatic upswing in value due to what is going on outside the community in the market. Also, make sure you understand that you can also have dramatic downswings in value to due to what is going on too can't you?

Think of it this way, the less an apartment community can be affected by outside force in the community the better. You are not looking for dramatic upswings in value even though you would take it. We are not looking to hit a home run the first time we are up to bat. We want to get on base and make great progress from there and the more insulated the property is from outside forces in that market – the better.

I had a client that purchased an apartment community in a market that was subject to dramatic swings in property values due to the types of businesses and companies that domiciled there. He decided to invest in an apartment community in this market because of the flood of economic activity at that time and all the optimistic predictions of even more business to come.

For the first three years he was rubbing my nose in this. He was getting over a 24% return on his money and was laughing about this all the way to the bank and reminding me every time I saw him. I was happy for him and glad it was working out so well.

Until…

About five years after he invested in the community, he called me and asked if I could help in the selling of the community. Surprised at the request I asked what was going on. He told me that the largest employer (by far) in the market had decided to move their production to another community. So, what was for a few years a very full community turned into a see-through apartment community.

By the time I got involved it was too late. I could not work my magic on this property enough to get it sold for him and the property ended up going back to the bank in foreclosure.

The crazy thing is that only a few years earlier it was doing unbelievable!

Now, think…you are an investor wanting to make the best decision. You may not have a lot of time left to grow your wealth. Will you choose a property that is not insulated from swings in value or will you choose a community that is pretty much insulated from sudden swings in value?

Look for insulated apartment communities.

EXISTING

Focus on existing apartment communities not new construction. Why? New construction costs more money. Now that I have made the most obvious statement you can imagine stay with me. Remember, cost of living? Remember that everyone must work? Well, as the cost of construction increases it will leave more and more potential renters behind and unable to rent these communities. Why? Because of the rent these communities will need to generate for the community to not only pay for those new construction dollars but also to give a decent return to its investors.

In short, residents will pay less rent to live in an existing community vs. a new one. As people find their money getting tighter and tighter where will most people gravitate to? Existing apartments.

Therefore, you want own existing now as this will be the "go to" investment for years to come. Investor demand will not be for new construction and will not be for conversions or high-rise properties. They will be for existing apartments and doesn't it make sense to put yourself in the path of what more and more investors will demand?

Remember, if you are 50 years or older this a key. To be in the path of demand and the path will be existing apartments and it is not only in the path of existing apartments it is the four items that I just mentioned that will give you the investment return and income you deserve:

Boring   Insulation   Existing   Predictable

Let these be your four keys to apartment community investment success.

*Quick FYI: Of course, there are always exceptions and to think that you cannot have apartment community investment success outside of the parameters I set in this chapter would be naive. However, if you do not have time for any mistakes then, this is the formula I recommend you follow.

Chapter 9

Using Apartment Communities To Blow Up Your IRA or 401(k)

Want to really maximize apartment community investing? Use your IRA to invest.

This makes a lot of sense for most people because this is where their largest "pile of money" is – their IRA or 401k.

Even though IRA/401k investing in real estate has been around for a number of years there are many investors that are not aware of this and not familiar with how to do this.

Some investors shy away from investing their IRA into a great apartment community because it sounds complicated. The great news is it is very easy to do and even better, you CAN invest your IRA in an apartment community as it is perfectly legitimate per the IRS as well!

Before I go any further let me tell you that I personally have my own 401k dollars that are invested in apartment communities! I don't just make recommendations I also walk the talk.

The first step in investing your IRA is to find an IRA custodian that allows you to "Self-Direct" your IRA investment. Simply put, "Self-Direct" means that you call the shots as to where your IRA dollars are invested by telling the custodian that houses your IRA where you want the money to be invested. This process not only allows you to invest in apartment communities but pretty much whatever else you want too! Of course, there are a handful of things that the IRS says you cannot invest your IRA into (I think art, stamps and rare coins are among them) but once you house your IRA moneys with a qualified IRA custodian you are off to the races. In fact, here are your easy steps to directing the investing of your IRA.

1. Check to see if the company that houses your IRA currently allows you to self-direct your investments giving you the ability to choose where your IRA is invested. If they do allow this talk to a representative at this company about investing some of your IRA moneys into an apartment community and what the process would be to do that. If your company does not allow you to self-direct and they (not you) decide where your IRA money is invested, then go to step 2.

2. Locate a Self-directed IRA Custodian. I will give you a couple of recommendations later in the chapter.

3. Have part or all your IRA transferred to the Self-directed IRA custodian. If your IRA is currently housed with a company that does not allow you to self-direct your IRA this is a simple paperwork exercise. It is a simple transfer from where your IRA is now to the Self-directed IRA custodian. The process will usually take about two weeks from beginning to end.

4. Once your IRA dollars are transferred to your new Self-directed custodian look for an apartment community to invest in. *Note: You do not have to wait until all of this is completed before you start looking for a good apartment community investment. You can also find an investment and commit to investing in a community first contingent upon getting this self-directed process completed. I have investment partners do this all the time.*

5. Once you find that apartment community to invest in complete the necessary paperwork that your custodian will require for the apartment community investment. Usually the custodian will want a copy of the apartment community investment Operating Agreement, Private Placement Memorandum or both as part of their processing. Again, this is an easy paperwork exercise to complete.

6. Once all of the documents are completed with your IRA Custodian your investment is made and now you can enjoy all of the benefits of owning that apartment community all tax deferred!

Again, this is a fairly easy process from A to Z and if you are not taking advantage of what the IRS will allow you are making a mistake. Plus, this allows you to direct your own investments vs. having some fat cat on Wall Street doing it for you.

Self-Directed IRA Custodians I Recommend:

Midland IRA
135 S. La Salle St.
Ste. 2150
Chicago, IL 60603
(312) 767-6863
www.midlandira.com

Millennium Trust Company
2001 Spring Road Ste 700
Oak Brook, IL 60523
(630) 368-5600
www.mtrustcompany.com

Right now, over 35% of our investment partners have some or all their IRA dollars invested in apartment communities. This IS an easy process but often an overlooked one. No matter your age this is worth every second you will spend looking into. Put your IRA or 401k on overdrive today!

Chapter 10

The Final Word On Apartment Community Investing And Your Financial Future

This book was really intended for those that are 50 years or older but the information easily applies to all investors.

It is funny, once you turn 50 you start to realize that you do not have that much time left to make smart financial decisions that will propel your wealth from where it is now to where you really want it to be. You can't take your time anymore. Now is the time to find the best investment you can based on what is happening not only economically but also politically and socially. Unfortunately, too many outside events impact how investment will not only perform over time but also the safety of these investments.

Throughout this book I have told you that there is a very strong case that apartment ownership and owning your very own apartment community (or communities) is where I see the biggest payoff for investors in the coming years. Yes, I am sticking my neck out there and predicting this to be the case, but I am also using information that is available to all investors. This is not some secret formula, this is not some algorithm that was invented, this is not mystery. This is real world information on what is not only happening now but what is to come.

As you decide to get more involved in the possibility of owning your own apartment community, I would recommend you connect with me and stay in touch with me as this is my mission. Not only do I provide weekly information on apartment community investments, state of the apartment and commercial real estate investment market but also provide information on real apartment communities to see, analyze and even invest in if you want. Thousands of investors are connected to me to get the latest updates and information on apartment investing and frankly this is where you should start your journey as well.

Simply go online to: www.daringarman.com

This simple web site will allow you to join our apartment investment community and get involved at whatever level you wish. You can simply hang around and see what it's all about, get my communications over email, take some classes and even ask some questions all the way to starting your investment in being an owner of your very own apartment community. You can get as serious about apartment community investing as you want by going to this web site. It is very easy to do.

Also, if you have questions about what you found in this book or want to explore apartment community investing even further you can send me a personal email at: darin@heartlandinvestmentpartners.com. Yes, this IS my email address and I do review and answer emails that come in. So, if you decide you want to communicate with me personally that would be great as well. As always, no obligation, no strings with me.

So here you are. You have reached the end of this book and I only have one more question for you:

If not now…when?

I hope you take advantage of what is to come and profit handsomely in the process. I look forward to hearing about your success story.

About Darin Garman

Starting his career out of college as a prison guard of all things, over 25 years ago Darin began his real estate investment experience as a real estate broker to leave his prison guard job. Since that time, Darin took the entrepreneurial path and has established himself as one of the nation's most "looked up to" experts in the world of apartments and commercial investment real estate. Since entering the world of commercial investment property Darin has been responsible for over $800,000,000 in apartment and investment property acquisitions and has become the "go to guy" for those looking for profitable long-term plays in conservative apartment investments. Darin has also raised over $70,000,000 in funds for different apartment investment properties.

Darin also has experience as a founding member of a startup bank – Family Merchants Bank of Cedar Rapids. Darin was one of the founding members and owners of this bank. In this capacity Darin not only was an owner but also sat on the banks Board of Directors and was a member of the bank's credit committee. Darin remained an owner and shareholder of the bank, remained on the Bank Board of Directors as well as on the Credit Committee until the bank was sold approximately three years later.

Not only is Darin very familiar with not only maximizing value and cash flow from investment real estate but also has an ownership interest in whole or in part in over $45,000,000 in apartment and commercial investment real estate throughout the heartland and is a guest on investment real estate panels, podcasts, seminars and investment radio talk shows. Darin also is an accomplished author including *"Getting Rich in Real Estate Partnerships"*, *"Paranoid Banker Secrets – A Conservative Investors Guide to Double Digit Returns in Any Economy"*, plus the *"The 9 Month Investment, A Passive Investors Guide to Achieving 10 Years of Wealth Accumulation in Only 9 Months"*. Also, Darin has been co-author of books such as - *"Wealth Attraction For Entrepreneurs...The No Holds Barred Kick Butt Guide To Becoming Rich"* with business and marketing guru Dan Kennedy.

Darin oversees the management of over 30 real estate partnerships as well as the properties owned by the partnerships on a day to day basis and is very familiar with what needs to be done as an investor and owner of these properties to maximize value and return for investors and owners.

Darin graduated from the University of Northern Iowa with a BA degree in Criminology 1989. Darin is originally from Algona, IA and currently lives and offices out of Marion, Iowa. Darin has been married for 30 years to Gina Garman and has three children, Madisen who is 26, Malory who is 22 and Isaiah who is 19.

More information on Darin can be found at:

www.daringarman.com;
www.heartlandinvestmentpartners.com;
www.theparanoidbanker.com;
www.9monthinvestment.com and
www.commercial-investments.com

There you will also find comments from clients of Darin, past and present.

Also, feel free to email Darin any of your questions or comments at **darin@heartlandinvestmentpartners.com**

www.ingramcontent.com/pod-product-compliance
Lightning Source LLC
Chambersburg PA
CBHW071438220526
45469CB00004B/1580